Business

Strategy

For Success

User Guide

Principles for Strategic Management of Business Initiatives, Projects and Programs

By Russell Freytag

Copyright

All rights reserved. No portion of this book may be reproduced, distributed, or transmitted by any process or technique without the express written consent of the publisher.

ISBN 10: 1985787563
ISBN 13: 978-1985787568
Library of Congress Control Number:
CreateSpace Independent Publishing Platform
North Charleston, South Carolina

Inquiries may be made at RussellFreytag2@gmail.com

CONTENTS

	Introduction	3
Step 1	Pain Management	6
Step 2	Current State of Business	10
Step 3	Symptoms	14
Step 4	The Problem	16
Step 5	High Level Strategy	18
Step 6	The Plan	20
Step 7	Management of Change	24
Step 8	Business Plan	26
Step 9	Your Target	28
Step 10	Support	30
Step 11	IT – The Data	32
Step 12	Features and Functionalities	34
Step 13	Business Requirements	36
	Demand Process Deliverables	37

INTRODUCTION

Step by Step checklist of Business Deliverables within the Strategic Life Cycle

The diagram below is an example of a strategic initiative software development project using the SDLC lifecycle. It illustrates how the *Business Fundamentals* flow into the SDLC framework. Smaller, or run rate, projects may utilize varying degrees of these steps depending on their complexity and scope.

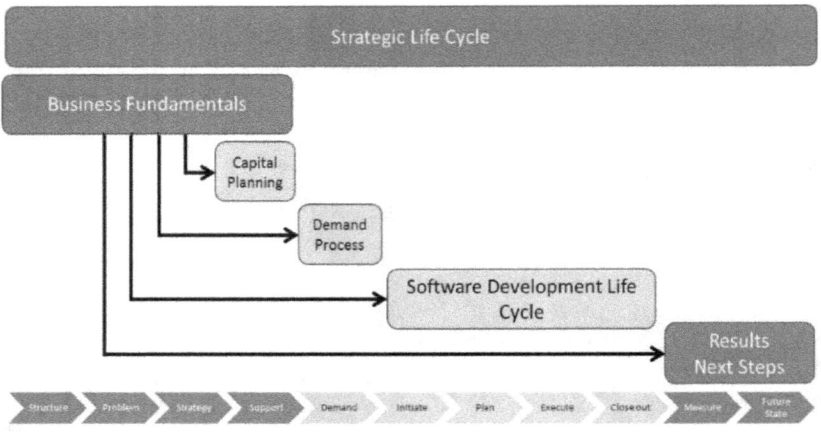

Strategy should be run as a project. The following list is a step by step checklist to create a strategy to prepare your next project. These steps are completed by the business and submitted to IT for development.

This example illustrates how the business fundamentals feed into the capital planning process and demand process resulting in projects generated with solid business requirements and clear scope. The IT project team will then deliver back to the business with measurable success criteria.

Planning Phase Project Plan Summary

1. Pain Management – How you are managing the pain today.
2. Business – Understand the current state of the business.
3. Symptoms – Identify the problem you are trying to solve.
4. The Problem – Identify the root cause of the problem.
5. Strategy – Identify the high-level strategy.
6. The Plan – Develop the future state detail plan.
7. Management of Change – Develop the change management plan.
8. Business Plan – Develop your business plan.
9. Your Target (Goals) – Create the end state.
10. Support – Gain executive support.
11. IT The Data – Validate your source data.
12. Features and Functionalities – Understand the features you want.
13. Business Requirements – Be able to describe to IT exactly what requirements need to be met.

Begin your project.

Step 1 Pain Management (Executive and Business Sponsor Step)

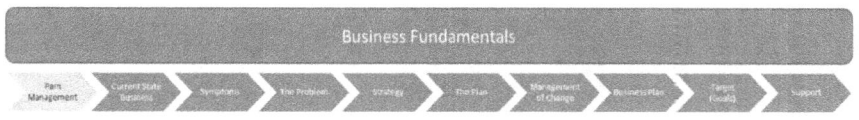

Roles; Executive Sponsor and Business Sponsor

How are you managing the *pain* today? Do you understand the current state of the business? These questions are designed to make you think about where you are and ask, "Can you be successful in your current state or do you need to make changes before you start your project?".

- Are you managing symptoms or are you looking for the root cause of the problems you are having today?

- How is your work occurring today? Are you proactive or reactive?

    - **Planning** - Are you spending time planning and setting defined goals that you carry out daily and weekly without fail?

    - **Direction** – Do you have clear direction from your executive team? Do you know exactly what your goals are and how the success of those goals will be measured?

    - **Strategy** – Has the strategy been communicated and are you are 100% clear on what the strategy is for this project? If you are not sure where you are going, no one else will know either. You will have failed before you started.

Current state of the company –

- Is the company experiencing rapid, flat, or negative growth?

    - Rapid growth can generate frequent structural, personnel, and technological changes. These rapid changes can make it challenging to progress.

    - Flat growth can generate frequent structural and personnel changes along with a highly competitive environment that may inhibit collaboration between teams.

    - Negative growth can cause layoffs and a negative work environment and moral.

Does the current structure support your objectives?

- Do you have the right people, processes, and technology to support your objectives?

    - People – do you have people with the right skillsets in your organization?

    - Processes – Have you documented the current state processes and identified the gaps that need to be addressed?

    - Technology – do you have the right technology to support your initiative?

Define the current state of the business

- What are the areas of the business that have gaps. Do these gaps need to be filled prior to starting your project?

Picking the right person for the project – page 2 *Business Strategy for Success*

- This is an important step. You need to pick the right person who aligns with the complexity, size, and experience needed to be successful in this role. The executive sponsor will need to work with this person daily, as needed, and be available with open and honest bidirectional communication. (Cards on the table communication)

Sponsors Role – Changing from how projects are run today to a strategic project will be a change that must be managed. This requires clear communication. As the executive sponsor you must be available to your project team, as needed, especially at the beginning of the project. You own the vision and gaining consensus with the team is important for complete alignment. Understanding among the executive sponsor and the project team is a must to avoid unrealistic decisions, deadlines, and timelines that are communicated up and imposed on the team.

Pain Management Pitfalls

- Not having executive communication, engagement, and support on the project.
- Not evaluating the current state of your company and business environment.
- Not picking the right person to run the project.

Step 2 Current State of the Business

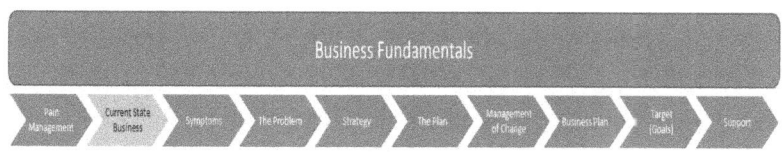

Understand the current state of the business

Identify the problem you are trying to solve

Identify the roles you will need for this project; Executive Sponsor, Business Sponsor, PM, Business Analyst, Process Engineer, Business SME's, IT Architect/Evangelist, Finance (CBA) Designate, Change Management Lead, Visionary (the person that pulls all the information together and creates the strategy), Business System Analyst, Data Analyst

Tools; Excel, Visio, One note

- Groups affected – Identify all the groups that will be affected by this project. Start by building an excel spreadsheet. The first tab will be Groups Impacted for the organizations, listing all managers and directors for each group.

- SME's for each group – From the managers you will begin to populate all SME's for each area and all one-off processes that may not be well known.

- Roles and responsibilities affected – Categorize all roles that are affected.

Gather information; Business Analyst role, continue excel spreadsheet, Process Engineer role, process mapping standardize format / content. Business Sponsor to help with analysis.

- Interviewing SME's from all groups affected (One note works well to take the notes and transcribe as much as possible) and transfer the issues into excel. Some sample column headings to start your analysis may include; Problems, Ranking, People Process Technology Structure, Buckets, Category, Needed Processes, Comments, Current State and Root Cause, (this is the last box to fill in). Keep in mind that analysis is subjective, so columns will change. Start with the problem column first, summarizing the issues that were communicated to you by the SME's.

- Be aware of what is being said as well as what is not being said. Probe with questions. What would you do? If you had your way, how would it work?

Process Mapping – Process Engineer role (highlight time, manual processes, pain points). This process mapping will identify the gaps that you need to address to fix processes. It will also help you in your analysis to find the root cause of the problems.

- Incorporate Time in motion studies where applicable – time in motion studies can be added to your CBA as hard benefits.

- Write out the current process steps – These steps are critical in determining the current state.

- Ask the SME's how it should work (prompt them with questions) – This is a second opportunity to work with the SME's and get their input. Remember, if you want them to work with you, you must earn their trust.

Review all test scripts for accuracy – If you don't have current test scripts this is an opportunity to update or create them. This is critical for an application project. You will not be able to test the changes or new system if you don't have test scripts complete for all groups, users, and one off uses for the application.

Take into consideration the current structure – (Business Analyst) As you are doing your analysis, continue to look at the structure and ask if it is set up to be successful.

Look at the big picture. Is it the right structure to be successful? Do we have the right people, process, technology, and business structure to be successful?

The objective is to understand all the pain points. (Symptoms)

Business Sponsors Role – Ensure that you have a good understanding of the current state of the business. Remember to engage throughout the project and educate yourself on the current state of the business to ensure that you make the right decisions. Join in the analysis of current state, process flows, time in motion, and the current structure. Help interpret all the information and set the direction for the team.

Current State Pitfalls

- Not gathering all issues with the current state.
- Not process mapping the current state.
- Not doing a time in motion study.

Step 3 Symptoms

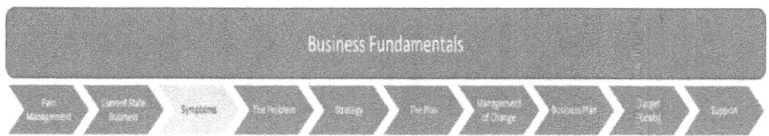

Dependencies – Pain Management, Current state

Roles; Executive Sponsor, Business Sponsor, PM, Business Analyst, Business SME's, Process Engineer, Visionary

Listen to ALL the problems people are experiencing.

Analysis of the information gathered

- Analyze the symptoms to understand the root cause of the problem.

- Categorize them into people, process, technology, and structure. (Excel spreadsheet you started earlier, Business Analyst)

- Continue to categorize into buckets until you find the structure. (rank your symptoms in excel)

- Add in current state and needed processes. (Excel, Business Analyst)

- Final step is to add root cause. Having the ability to view a lot of information, proposed solutions, and buckets of work. Go from high level to detail to help you figure out the root cause of the issue or issues. It may be a single cause or many causes.

Business Sponsors Role – Guide the team to the root cause of the problem. You should be building consensus along the way. Work with the team to review the information. You should be involved with the team through this process.

Symptom Pitfalls

- Not doing the analysis of all issues with the current state.

Step 4 The Problem

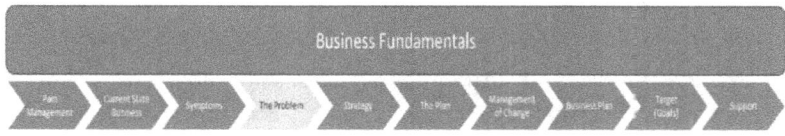

Dependencies – **Pain Management, Current state, Symptoms**

Roles; Executive Sponsor, Business Sponsor, PM, Business Analyst, Business SME's, Process Engineer, Visionary

Identify the root cause of the problems.

Define the root cause of the problems. (Excel)

- There may be many causes that take time, money, or technology to solve. Categorize the problems into things that you can fix immediately, things that are mid-term, and finally long-term fixes that will take time and budget.

- You may have to escalate to your executive team to help resolve some issues. These are your mid and long-term solutions.

- Identify risk associated with both solving the problem and not solving the problem. What will it cost to fix these issues or ask the question, "What if we do nothing?".

Lock on the problem or problems you are trying to solve. (Business Analyst, Business Sponsor)

- You cannot move forward without a clear statement of the problem you will be solving.

Business Sponsors Role – Guide the team to the root cause of the problem. You should be building consensus along the way and leading the team through this process.

The Problem Pitfalls

- Not identifying the root cause problem or problems.

Step 5 High Level Strategy

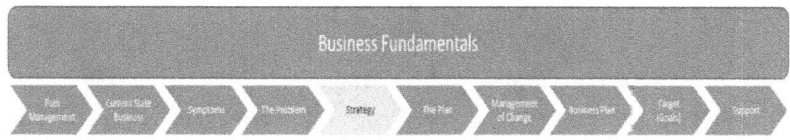

Identify the high-level Strategy you will use.

Dependencies – **Pain Management, Current state, Symptoms, Root Cause of the Problem, Risk**

Roles; Executive Sponsor, Business Sponsor, PM, Business Analyst, Process Engineer, Business SME's, IT Architect/Evangelist, Finance (CBA) Designate, Visionary

Analyze the buckets of work you gathered from defining the problem. (Make notation of the things you can control, escalations to executive team, items that require budget considerations and leadership alignment)

- **People** – Do you need new roles, additional people, reallocation of resources? Develop future state roles and do the gap analysis, current to future state.

- **Process** – Define what processes need to change. For example; cost, role changes, and automation. Develop your future state processes. Do the gap analysis and the current state to future state analysis.

- **Technology** – Are you condensing the time it takes to do every task? Validate the cost and time in motion study with all parties. Define current to future state technology.

- **Structure** – Define the future state business structure, validate cost, people, and roles. Do the gap analysis.

Create your strategy based on the facts above.

- First create your high-level strategic plan. Include a roadmap of what you are going to deliver with high level timelines and t-shirt sizing cost.

- Validate with finance (finance CBA designate), your manager and sponsors for viability and to gain alignment.

Business Sponsors Role – This is your strategy. You should define what success looks like. Think about the concentric rings. What are the problems you are going to work on? Define the future state of your business during this process.

Strategy Pitfalls

- Not breaking analysis into short, medium, and long term-goals.
- Not creating a high-level strategy and validating it with the sponsors, management, and finance.

Step 6 The Plan

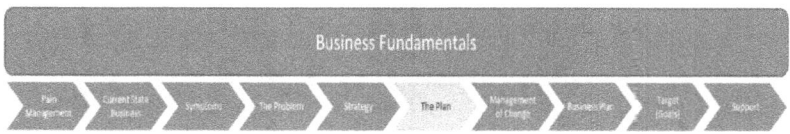

Develop the detail plan

Dependencies – Pain Management, Current State, Symptoms, Root Cause of the Problem, Risk, High Level Strategy

Roles; Executive Sponsor, Business Sponsor, PM, Business Analyst, Process Engineer, Business SME's, IT Architect/Evangelist, Finance (CBA) Designate, Visionary, Change Management Lead

Define exactly what the end state will look like. This takes collaboration between many areas. You will need to go back to the teams affected by the change to ensure that you have designed a solution that works for them.

Analysis – This is the deep dive to identify what will need to change from current to future state. You will need to present this analysis to your Executive Sponsor to gain their support and present these recommendations to the higher-tiered executives who have approval over structural changes. These changes are usually realized at the end of the project which can create conflict. Use the high-level strategy you completed to create the detailed state whiteboard. This piece sets you up for change management and helps align the roles that are changing and creating buy-in from the teams that are effected.

- **Structural changes** – Will the structure change? Identify what the changes are and create your recommendations for future state. Is ownership moving from one area to another? Are you changing technology (applications)?

- **Groups impacted** – Will the teams in current state be changed by the future state? If so, make sure to notate that information in detail for discussion with your executive sponsor.

- **Roles and responsibilities** – Define all role changes and notate potential new roles for the people affected by this change.

- **Processes** – Continue development of your detailed future state processes. These are your white board processes that you will be working through with the teams for feasibility.

Design new processes, teams, and roles – continue development of end state.

- **Work with your technical evangelist** – On any technology changes, new applications needs, and manual to automated solutions.

- **Recommendations from SME's** – Make sure you are meeting with SME's, not just in groups but one on one, especially with people who are key to your project. Sometimes you will find one SME that knows the entire end to end process. This person will be invaluable to you as you move forward.

- **Create your future state** – You should now have your future state created with input from all teams, the business, and IT.

Validate the new strategy with all teams – Check point:

- Does it work for all teams – with all Business Groups
- Do all teams have measurable gains – with Finance CBA Designate
- Architecturally is it sound – with IT Evangelist
- Validate / alignment – with Executive Sponsors

Business Sponsors Role – You should be driving the analysis and developing this plan with the team.

The Plan Pitfalls

- Not creating a detailed plan of the end state. (people, process, technology and structure)

Step 7 Management of Change

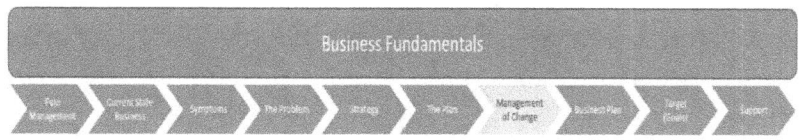

Develop the Change Management Plan

Dependencies – **Pain Management, Current State, Symptoms, Root Cause of the Problem, Risk, High-Level Strategy**, Future State Plan

Roles; Executive Sponsor, Business Sponsor, PM, Business Analyst, Process Engineer, Business SME's, IT Architect/Evangelist, Finance (CBA) Designate, Visionary, Change Management Lead

Change management lead identified – Bring this person up to speed on the project and keep them informed as you move forward.

Analysis

- Make sure all parties had input and validated the new processes. This is critical. It means the difference between adoption of the new processes and rejection.
- Review / Analyze changes in current to future state processes.

Identify all changes and put them into buckets (this will help in your analysis)

- People – Identify all groups, teams, people, and roles.
- Processes – Identify all processes that are changing.
- Technology – Identify applications, infrastructure, HW, and SW.
- Structural – Identify Data migration, financial / reporting data, and customer Information. (PHI, Billing, Payment information)

Create the Change Management Plan - timing, training, and managing the transition of the changes

- Manage all transitions and clear the path for changes to be successful.
- Identify any roadblocks and work with the sponsor to resolve any issues.

Validation with all teams the full change management plan

- All teams know their new roles and processes are defined and validated. This is critical for adoption of the new roles and processes.

Business Sponsors Role – Your responsibility is to identify the changes and make sure you have a plan to manage the politics around all changes.

Management of Change Pitfalls

- Not incorporating a change management lead into the project.
- Not validating the future state plan with all teams and executives to gain support.

Step 8 Business Plan

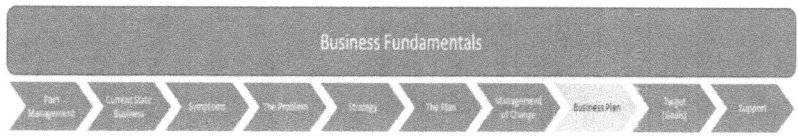

Develop your Business Plan

Dependencies – Pain Management, Current State, Symptoms, Root Cause of the Problem, Risk, High Level Strategy, Future State Plan, Change Management Plan

Roles; Executive Sponsor, Business Sponsor, PM, Business Analyst, Process Engineer, Business SME's, IT Architect/Evangelist, Finance (CBA) Designate, Visionary, Change Management Lead

Finance designate to provide guidance / advice on all elements of cost.

- Alignment with corporate initiatives.

- Root cause of the problem. What if we do nothing? (Cost)

- Current state cost. (operational, headcount, growth impacts)

- Time in motion and other measurements. (reduced headcount, automation etc.)

- Cost of interim and future state. (changes and impact)

- Validate/manage the change management plan.
- Validate, provide guidance on the CBA and ROI.
- Provide guidance and assist/validate with the one-page executive summary.
  - **Cost of the strategy** (include options if appropriate)

Business Sponsors Role – Your responsibility to manage / direct the team on the development of the financial plan. This is how you will measure the success of your strategy. Be sure to validate this plan with your finance designate before moving forward. If you are not familiar with the elements that go into a business plan, you will need to educate yourself on these.

Business Plan Pitfalls

- Not incorporating a finance designate into the project to keep the business plan realistic and aligned to corporate initiatives.

Step 9 Your Target (Goals)

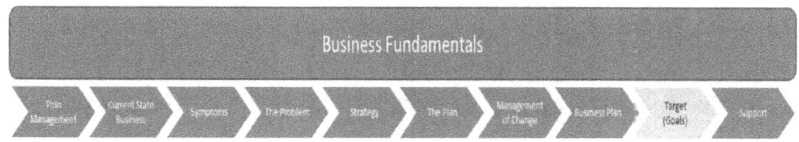

Create the End State

Dependencies – Pain Management, Current State, Symptoms, Root Cause of the Problem, Risk, High Level Strategy, Future State Plan, Change Management Plan, Business Plan, CBA, ROI

Roles; Executive Sponsor, Business Sponsor, PM, Business Analyst, Process Engineer, Business SME's, IT Architect/Evangelist, Finance (CBA) Designate, Visionary, Change Management Lead

You now have all the information you need to define your end state

Create your concentric rings

- Define the problem statement.
- Define the strategy.
- Define the future state.
- Change management plan.
- CBA.

- ROI.

- Create your strategy, roadmap, and timelines.

- Define your success criteria.

These are the items you are going to use to measure success.

Business Sponsors Role – It is your responsibility to create these deliverables. They are the tools you will communicate to the executive team to convey the problem, the plan, and what you expect to gain from this effort. These fundamentals will feed your capital planning process, demand process, and the SDLC process.

Target Goals Pitfalls

- Not defining the end state with strategy, financials, roadmap, and success criteria.

Step 10 Support

Dependencies – Pain Management, Current State, Symptoms, Root Cause of the Problem, Risk, High Level Strategy, Future State Plan, Change Management Plan, Business Plan, CBA, ROI Roadmap and Timelines

Roles; Executive Sponsor, Business Sponsor, PM, Business Analyst, Process Engineer, Business SME's, IT Architect/Evangelist, Finance (CBA) Designate, Visionary, Change Management Lead

The information you developed will help you garner executive support for your business development strategy.

- Problem statement.
- High Level Strategy.
- Strategy roadmap / timeline.
- One-page executive summary with financials.
- ROI.

Back up.

- CBA.
- Change management plan.
- Current and future state of the business.

Business Sponsors Role – Clear, concise communication upward will help you cut through the politics and drive fact-based decisions.

Support Pitfalls

- Not gaining executive support for your strategy.

CAPITAL PLANNING DELIVERABLES ARE COMPLETE

Planning and preparation will lead to a higher success of support and funding during the Capital Planning Process.

The following steps will help you prepare for your project and are an input into the demand process.

Step 11 IT The Data Chapter 7 in the book

Roles; Executive Sponsor, Business Sponsor, PM, IT Architect/Evangelist, Visionary, Change Management Lead, Business System Analyst, Data Analyst

New Role Data analyst is key to all software projects.

- Centralize Data within the Team.
- Tie the Data Analyst and the business sponsor (business product manager) together.
- Have control over the data.
- Create a dataflow that is fully defined and mapped out.
- Have all calculations validated, approved, and published.
- Set up the foundation correctly to achieve the strategic objectives.
- Create a "Cave" or place for the team to work together.

Blend Business Process into Technology

Document current to future state technical flows

Sponsors Role – You own this product. The most important element in a software project is the data. It is your responsibility to ensure you have a person that is responsible for getting clean data, organizing and storing the data, calculating and displaying the correct information, utilizing the best technology, and making your product scalable and transferable to any business or organization you acquire or expand into.

IT The Data Pitfalls

- Not incorporating a data analyst into the project.
- Not centralizing the data to the team.

Step 12 Features and Functionalities Chapter 5 in the book

Roles; Executive Sponsor, Business Sponsor, PM, IT Architect/Evangelist, Business Analyst, Visionary

The high-level strategy (Step 5) and the plan (Step 6) give you the Features and Functionalities.

- Validation with all business partners needs and priorities.
- Validation of current state of the business.
- Validation of current state processes for all groups affected.
- Validation of current state roles and responsibilities for all functional groups.

Define the integration plan;

- Roles and responsibilities.
- Executive support across all groups.
- Change management plan.
- Communication across all groups.

Sponsors Role – You own the management of change for this project. Front end work of clear communication and validation with all groups on the plan and changes that are planned and coming to all groups and their impact to these teams is key to the success of the project. Look for any issues and resistance to change and address it early.

Symptoms

- You cannot identify all the groups, SME's, current state of the business, current state processes, roles & responsibilities, as well as features and functionalities. You need to evaluate any steps you missed and complete them before moving forward.

Features and Functionalities Pitfalls.

- Not evaluating what was missed. If you are having trouble defining the features and functionalities for the project, this can result in technical debt that you may not be able to overcome in the future.

Step 13 Business Requirements Chapter 6 in the book

Roles; Executive Sponsor, Business Sponsor, PM, Business Analyst, IT Architect/Evangelist, Visionary

You can pull the business requirements from the features and functionalities (Step 12).

- Validation with IT to ensure what is being asked for and what will be delivered are aligned.
- Business integration with IT to write the BRD. Make sure you are getting questions out of the way now. Alignment between the teams in what is asked for and what is being built.
- Formal (Standardized) documenting future state processes and gap analysis.
- Formal defining future state roles and responsibilities.
- Develop risk management plan.
  - **Ready to start your project.**

Symptoms

- You are having trouble defining your business requirements

Business Requirements Pitfalls

- Not clearly and cleanly defining your business requirements.

Business Sponsors Role – Ensure that you have completed the work to create a successful project

DEMAND PROCESS DELIVERABLES ARE COMPLETE

Business fundamentals and planning are the foundational elements that feed the capital process, demand process, and SDLC. This enables you to measure the program/project results and determine the next steps.

If you have not completed all the steps, you risk creating more unplanned work (technical debt) than you can resolve. This can result in the ultimate failure of the program. The programs will fail or perform poorly because the steps in this user guide have not been completed.

Example below

Projects run without Strategy

Work continues to increase through launch. If the project makes it to launch? You still have to do the work and it takes longer.

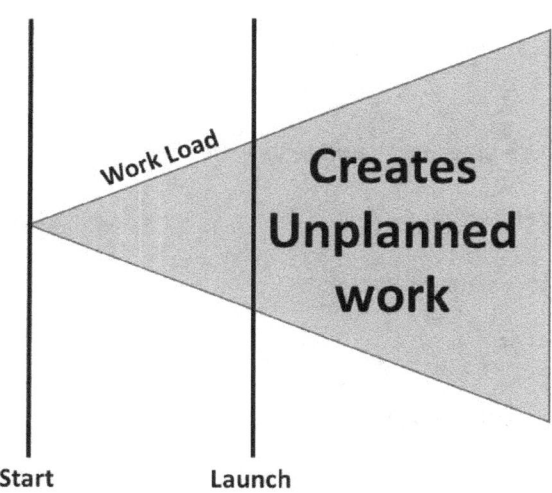

A project that has completed all the steps will work as intended and the result will look like the example below allowing for the final steps of measure and future state to be worked on as illustrated on page one of the guide.

Projects run with Strategy

Increase the rate of success by 50%

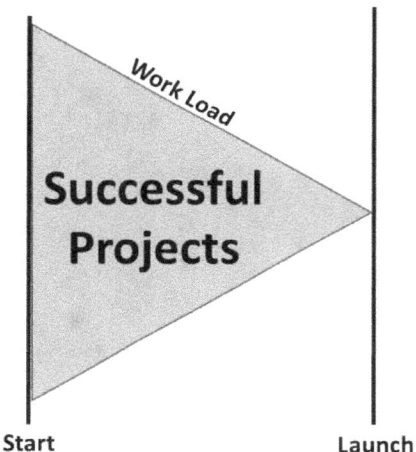

These are the high-level elements that go into creating a strategy. I hope you find this user guide helpful in your future endeavors.

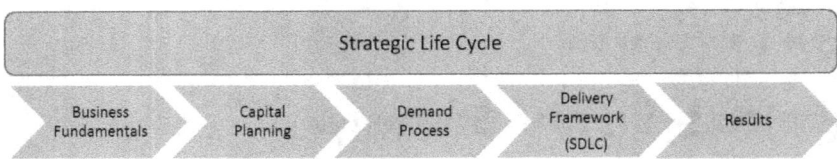

www.ingramcontent.com/pod-product-compliance
Lightning Source LLC
Chambersburg PA
CBHW030059230526
45471CB00003B/1167